CHRISTIANITY 101

THINGS YOU WISH YOUR PASTOR TOLD YOU

JACOB ENGLISH

Without limiting the rights under copyright(s) reserved below, no part of this publication may be reproduced, stored in, or introduced into a retrieval system, or transmitted, in any form, or by any means (electronic, mechanical, photocopying, recording, or otherwise) without the prior permission of the publisher and the copyright owner.

The content of this book is provided "AS IS." The Publisher and the Author make no guarantees or warranties as to the accuracy, adequacy, or completeness of or results to be obtained from using the content of this book, including any information that can be accessed through hyperlinks or otherwise, and expressly disclaim any warranty expressed or implied, including but not limited to implied warranties of merchantability or fitness for a particular purpose. This limitation of liability shall apply to any claim or cause whatsoever, whether such claim or cause arises in contract, tort, or otherwise. In short, you, the reader, are responsible for your choices and the results they bring.

The scanning, uploading, and distributing of this book via the internet or any other means without the publisher's and copyright owner's permission is illegal and punishable by law. Please purchase only authorized copies, and do not participate in or encourage piracy of copyrighted materials. Your support of the author's rights is appreciated.

Copyright © 2021 by Jacob English. All rights reserved.

Unless otherwise identified, Scripture quotations are taken from the Holy Bible, King James Version.

Book design by eBook Prep
www.ebookprep.com

June 2022
ISBN: 978-1-664457-307-5

Rise UP Publications
644 Shrewsbury Commons Ave
Ste 249
Shrewsbury PA 17361
United States of America
www.riseUPpublications.com
Phone: 866-846-5123

CONTENTS

Introduction	7
1. Who is God?	9
2. Who is Jesus?	11
3. Who is the Holy Spirit?	15
4. What Is Heaven?	17
5. What Is The Rapture?	19
6. What Is Hell?	21
7. What Is Sin?	23
8. What Is Sexual Immorality?	25
9. What Does It Mean To Be Saved?	27
10. How Do I Get Saved?	29
11. Can I Lose My Salvation?	45
12. What Is Holiness?	47
13. What Is The Baptism Of The Holy Ghost?	49
14. What Is Speaking In Tongues?	53
15. What Are The Gifts Of The Spirit?	59
16. What Is The Fruit Of The Spirit?	61
17. How Do I Deal With Difficult Situations In Life?	63
18. How Do I Overcome An Addiction?	65
19. How Do I Deal With Temptation?	67
20. What Are The Benefits Of Living For Christ?	69
21. What Is My Purpose?	73
22. How Do I Implement God's Will Into My Life Daily?	77
23. Is It Always God's Will To Deliver And Heal?	79
24. Is It God's Will For Me To Prosper?	81
25. What Is A Tithe and Why Does it Matter?	83
26. How Do I Pray?	87
27. What Is Faith?	89
28. Call To Repentance: Benediction	91
About the Author	95

To my Grandfather and mentor in the faith,

Phillip English.

INTRODUCTION

Many questions arise as to what the Bible has to say about life and how to live in a manner pleasing to God. This book is meant to give simple scriptural insight based on the questions we have all faced as new believers or simply by growing in faith. Whatever the question, the Bible has an answer for it. Through this book, you will receive biblical clarity and hopefully a renewed faith in God and his plan to reveal his love to you throughout your pursuit of him. May God continue to draw you closer to him.

1

WHO IS GOD?

> And Moses said unto God, Behold, when I come unto the children of Israel, and shall say unto them, The God of your fathers hath sent me unto you; and they shall say to me, What is his name? What shall I say unto them? And God said unto Moses, I AM THAT I AM: and he said, Thus shalt thou say unto the children of Israel, I AM hath sent me unto you.
>
> — EXODUS 3:13-14

God, our Father, is "Jehovah—the Unchangeable One". He created all that we know and all that we see and don't see (Genesis 1). He creates and has a will for every life, as He said to Jeremiah…

> Before I formed thee in the belly I knew thee; and before thou camest forth out of the womb I sanctified thee, and I ordained thee a prophet unto the nations.
>
> — JEREMIAH 1:5

God controls all things, and His plan will be completed. We understand through Adam's sin that although God had a plan for Adam, God gives man the ability to decide what we are going to do with our life. Through this ability, He also had a plan for us through Jesus to redeem us. God has a plan; there is nothing you can do to cancel His plan. The only thing we can do is decide whether we will be a part of His plan or not. God is Alpha and Omega—He formed the beginning from the end (Isaiah 46:10). He will not change His will. He will not do things our way. He is the Unchangeable One. What He says, is.

Understanding this simple truth allows us to approach God the right way, through submission. When we submit to God as our Father and to Jesus as our Lord, God will bless us as His children and joint-heirs with Jesus Christ.

2

WHO IS JESUS?

In the beginning was the Word, and the Word was with God, and the Word was God. He was in the beginning with God. All things were made through Him, and without Him nothing was made that was made. In Him was life, and the life was the light of men. And the light shines in the darkness, and the darkness did not comprehend it.

— JOHN 1:1-5 (NKJV)

And the Word became flesh and dwelt among us, and we beheld His glory, the glory as of the only begotten of the Father, full of grace and truth.

— JOHN 1:14 (NKJV)

Jesus is the living word of God. He is part of the Trinity; an equal part of the Godhead. He is God in every aspect as well as man in every aspect. He was born of a virgin, meaning that man's sin was not passed in His conception. He was conceived in Mary by the Holy Spirit, born without sin, and lived the first and only sinless life.

Jesus is God's only begotten Son (John 3:16). His purpose in life was to show us how we are supposed to live, what we are supposed to do as God's children on the earth, and ultimately, to die for the sins of mankind and save as many as will call on Him (John 1:12).

We could never pay the price for our sin without eternal damnation, but Jesus, being sinless, gave His life to pay the price of our sins (Romans 6:23). He took on the punishment of all sin on the cross of Calvary (John 19). Because He is the sinless living word of God, He could not be bound to death. Instead, Jesus broke the curse of death and took dominion from sin and Satan on the earth.

> *I am He who lives, and was dead, and behold, I am alive forevermore. Amen. And I have the keys of Hades and of Death.*
>
> — REVELATION 1:18 (NKJV)

Jesus paid the price for our sin for us to again freely have a relationship with God the Father through the Holy Spirit.

> *Jesus said to him, "I am the way, the truth, and the life. No one comes to the Father except through Me."*
>
> — JOHN 14:6 (NKJV)

Jesus, the Lamb of God, the Word, the Son of God, the Prince of Peace, the Lover of Our Soul! Finding Him and following Him is the heart of the believer. Our love for Jesus will be what keeps us in the walk of faith until we get to meet Him in eternity.

3

WHO IS THE HOLY SPIRIT?

> Nevertheless I tell you the truth. It is to your advantage that I go away; for if I do not go away, the Helper will not come to you; but if I depart, I will send Him to you.
>
> — JOHN 16:7 (NKJV)

> But ye shall receive power, after that the Holy Ghost is come upon you: and ye shall be witnesses unto me both in Jerusalem, and in all Judaea, and in Samaria, and unto the uttermost part of the earth.
>
> — ACTS 1:8

The Holy Spirit of God is the embodiment of holiness, the third part of the Trinity, the breath of God. He is who was taken from us when Adam sinned. Throughout the Old Testament, the Holy Spirit could come upon chosen people of God, but could not dwell in His temple. We are His temple!

> Know ye not that ye are the temple of God, and that the Spirit of God dwelleth in you?
>
> — 1 CORINTHIANS 3:16

When Jesus gave His life for us, mankind was enabled through Christ to again be filled with the Holy Spirit. The Holy Spirit entered into the body of Jesus after His death and brought Him to life again. He has come to us so that as we die to our old way of living, He can quicken us and help us live a new and holy life unto God.

> But if the Spirit of him that raised up Jesus from the dead dwell in you, he that raised up Christ from the dead shall also quicken your mortal bodies by his Spirit that dwelleth in you.
>
> — ROMANS 8:11

4

WHAT IS HEAVEN?

In my Father's house are many Mansions. If it were not so, would I have told you that I go to prepare a place for you?

— JOHN 14:2 (ESV)

He will wipe away every tear from their eyes, and death shall be no more, neither shall there be mourning, nor crying, nor pain anymore, for the former things have passed away.

— REVELATION 21:4 (ESV)

And the twelve gates were twelve pearls, each of the gates made of a single pearl, and the street of the city was pure gold, transparent as glass. And I saw no temple in the city, for its temple is the Lord God the Almighty and the Lamb. And the city has no need of sun or moon to shine on it,

> for the glory of God gives it light, and its lamp is the Lamb. By its light will the nations walk, and the kings of the earth will bring their glory into it, and its gates will never be shut by day—and there will be no night there.
>
> — REVELATION 21:21-25 (ESV)

Heaven is the eternal destination for the believer. It is the place where Jesus dwells at the right hand of the Father, and He prepares a place for us there. In heaven, there is no sickness or pain; there is no death or sorrow or sin. We are in the presence of the Almighty forever.

Imagine the most intense presence of God you have ever felt. We will be forever in the personal presence of God for eternity. We will be consumed with joy and freedom forever. Above all, we will be with the love of our life, Jesus Christ. What a wonderful thing to look forward to as a believer and a child of God.

5

WHAT IS THE RAPTURE?

The word "rapture" comes from the word "harpazo" in the Greek. When translated into Latin, it becomes the word "rapturo", which is where we derive the word "rapture" from.

This term is defined as being "caught up" and referred to as the "Great Catching Away".

> Behold, I tell you a mystery: We shall not all sleep, but we shall all be changed— in a moment, in the twinkling of an eye, at the last trumpet. For the trumpet will sound, and the dead will be raised incorruptible, and we shall be changed. For this corruptible must put on incorruption, and this mortal must put on immortality.
>
> — 1 CORINTHIANS 15:51-53

> For the Lord himself shall descend from heaven with a shout, with the voice of the archangel, and with

> the trump of God: and the dead in Christ shall rise first: Then we which are alive and remain shall be caught up together with them in the clouds, to meet the Lord in the air: and so shall we ever be with the Lord.
>
> — 1 THESSALONIANS 4:16-17

The Rapture is a time every believer looks forward to when Jesus Christ will return for all Christians, both dead and alive. As the scripture describes, he will resurrect those who are asleep (dead) and then call us who are alive to meet Him in the air. We will then be with Him in heaven in a new and glorified body, exiting time and entering eternity.

6

WHAT IS HELL?

> Whoever makes a practice of sinning is of the devil, for the devil has been sinning from the beginning. The reason the Son of God appeared was to destroy the works of the devil.
>
> — 1 JOHN 3:8 (ESV)

Hell is a destination not created for mankind but for Satan and his followers (Matthew 25:41). It is described as a lake of fire (Revelation 21:8) and as a bottomless pit, throughout the book of The Revelation.

The Bible declares that if you live in sin, you do not belong to God but are followers of the Devil.

We are all on a predestined path towards hell, and without Christ, we will finish our course there. Thanks be unto God our Father that He sent His Son, Jesus, so we wouldn't have to perish, but we can enter into life with Him (John 3:16).

Understanding the Gospel means realizing that God doesn't send anyone to hell. Hell is a destination for sin. Satan and his angels will go to hell because they are eternally bound in their sin. We have a great opportunity, a gift, given by the life and death of Jesus to become saved and not enter into eternal damnation. The only way to avoid hell is to be rid of sin.

Adam brought sin into the world and onto mankind. God didn't have anything to do with bringing sin on mankind, but God has everything to do with redeeming us from sin and saving us from hell. He can return us to our original state of dominion and life with Him by believing in His Son, Jesus.

7

WHAT IS SIN?

> Therefore to him that knoweth to do good, and doeth it not, to him it is sin.
>
> — JAMES 4:17

Sin can be defined simply as disobedience to God. It was Adam's sin that put a curse on mankind. Sin always carries side effects. We never know how far it will take us, but we know it will certainly always take us farther than we want to go.

If you read 1 John 3, you find that sin is always the separator of God and man. When you follow Christ, you turn your back on sin. We can't live a sinful lifestyle and please God. We can't live a sinful lifestyle and be saved.

8

WHAT IS SEXUAL IMMORALITY?

But the cowardly, unbelieving, abominable,
   murderers, sexually immoral, sorcerers, idolaters,
   and all liars shall have their part in the lake
   which burns with fire and brimstone, which is the
   second death.

   — REVELATION 21:8 (NKJV)

Do you not know that the unrighteous will not inherit
   the kingdom of God? Do not be deceived.
   Neither fornicators, nor idolaters, nor adulterers,
   nor homosexuals, nor sodomites, nor thieves, nor
   covetous, nor drunkards, nor revilers, nor
   extortioners will inherit the kingdom of God.

   — 1 CORINTHIANS 6:9-10 (NKJV)

In these two scriptures, we understand that no one will go to heaven being a participant of those sinful lifestyles. Knowing this, we also understand that it is not God's will to reject us because of our sins, but to take our sins away so that we are no longer found living in sin…instead justified, living a holy life by the power of the Holy Spirit and the blood of Jesus which washes us clean.

9

WHAT DOES IT MEAN TO BE SAVED?

> For I have been crucified with Christ, now I no longer live but Christ lives within me.
>
> — GALATIANS 2:20 (NIV)

The need for salvation stemmed from man's downfall in the garden of Eden. Adam and Eve, God's first created man and woman, partook of the fruit from the tree of knowledge of good and evil which God forbade them to eat, committing the first sin. Because of Adam's sin through disobedience, God's relationship with mankind was tainted, and God could no longer walk with mankind as He did in the garden of Eden. To restore His relationship with mankind, there had to be a blood sacrifice. God told Adam…

> The day that you eat of the fruit, you will surely die.
>
> — GENESIS 2:17

He instituted this by slaying the first beast (Genesis 3:21), and later through His covenant with the Hebrews through Moses, which He called the "Day of Atonement". This, along with the Levitical Law, was created to have a relationship with God (Exodus 19-24). Albeit, not the same relationship as before. Mankind was guilty. Because of Adam, we are all born into sin as the Bible says…

> For all have sinned and fall short of the glory of God.
>
> — ROMANS 3:23

We were eternally separated from our Father and unfit to receive His Spirit, and so we were dead in spirit. This is why we need a Savior. Without Jesus, we are doomed eternally to hell and the lake of fire created for Satan and his demons (Revelation 21:8). Thank God, He didn't leave us doomed. He sent Jesus.

When you receive Jesus as your Lord and Savior (Romans 10:9-10), you are born again (John 3:3-5). This means that although you were born in sin, you are a new creation born into life, a child of God!

Being saved means that who you were is dead, and now you belong to God. You have repented of your sin and now are living a life of joy, directed by the Holy Spirit of God.

10

HOW DO I GET SAVED?

REPENT AND BE CONVERTED

> Repent ye therefore, and be converted, that your sins may be blotted out, when the times of refreshing shall come from the presence of the Lord.
>
> — ACTS 3:19

Here we see that repentance and converting are keys to becoming saved.

Repentance means in Greek: "a change of heart or to turn away from". Repentance puts sin under the blood. Modern definition: "I'm sorry". Repentance is not merely sorrow. Being sorry brings you to repentance. Repentance means to change.

> For godly sorrow produces repentance leading to salvation.
>
> — 2 CORINTHIANS 7:10A (NKJV)

There must be repentance from sin to be saved. We cannot just be sorry about sin. We have to repent of it. How do I know this?

> Jesus answered them, "Truly, truly, I say to you, everyone who practices sin is a slave to sin.
>
> — JOHN 8:34 (ESV)

If we live in sin, we serve sin. If we are saved, we serve Jesus. Can we serve both?

> No man can serve two masters: for either he will hate the one, and love the other; or else he will hold to the one, and despise the other. Ye cannot serve God and mammon.
>
> — MATTHEW 6:24

> And Jesus answered him, It is written, You shall worship the Lord your God, and him only shall you serve.
>
> — LUKE 4:8 (ESV)

To be saved, we must turn from sin. This isn't saying we never sin. It is saying we don't live in a constant state of sin. We are turning away from it. We are leaving those things, those sins, behind and turning our back on them. We follow Jesus now.

> My little children, these things write I unto you, that ye sin not. And if any man sin, we have an advocate with the Father, Jesus Christ the righteous:
>
> — 1 JOHN 2:1

> Wherefore seeing we also are compassed about with so great a cloud of witnesses, let us lay aside every weight, and the sin which doth so easily beset us, and let us run with patience the race that is set before us,
>
> — HEBREWS 12:1

Knowing this, we can clearly see if we are a servant of sin we can't be a servant of Christ. We can only serve one.

> Whoever makes a practice of sinning is of the devil, for the devil has been sinning from the beginning. The reason the Son of God appeared was to destroy the works of the devil.
>
> — 1 JOHN 3:8 (ESV)

Sin is a work of the Devil. We don't live by sin, we live by faith. We cannot live by both.

> Now the just shall live by faith: but if any man draw back, my soul shall have no pleasure in him.
>
> — HEBREWS 10:38

BELIEVE AND CONFESS

> If thou shalt confess with thy mouth the Lord Jesus, and shalt believe in thine heart that God hath raised him from the dead, thou shalt be saved. For with the heart man believeth unto righteousness; and with the mouth confession is made unto salvation.
>
> — ROMANS 10:9-10

Here we see that belief and confession are required on our part. If you do "such and such" I will give you "such and such". This is a conditional gift, leaving the decision in our hands. So we understand: salvation is a decision.

There is an action required on our part to even start out our journey as a Christian as defined in the scriptures. We make a decision to serve Jesus with our life within our heart. Then, we confess Him as our Lord with our mouth. The idea that we don't have to do anything in ourselves to be saved stops right here, because we already see an action required on our behalf to be saved. Even though salvation is a gift, we can't be saved without doing these things. We have requirements.

Salvation is from God, we know that. It will be forever an irrevocable gift, always available to a living person. No one can take the gift away. That is not in question. We didn't earn it; it is a gift. We know that as well. The question is: Do you forcibly receive salvation or do you decide to receive it, and if you can decide to receive it, can you decide to walk away from it?

This is where we often hear the scripture...

> I give them eternal life, and they will never perish, and no one will snatch them out of my hand.
>
> — JOHN 10:28 (ESV)

Neglecting the gravity of the previous scripture...

> My sheep hear my voice, and I know them, and they follow me.
>
> — JOHN 10:27 (ESV)

Following Christ is a prerequisite to not being taken away. Wouldn't it then be concluded that we have chosen to leave His hand if we stop following Him?

If we decide to receive salvation, then can't we also decide not to? We learn that salvation is indeed based on our decisions in this basic truth. The fact stands. We decide that we want Jesus as our Lord, and we are saved, and then we confess that we belong to Him. Receiving the gift of salvation IS a decision.

Jesus died so that all people could be saved, right?

> For God so loved the world, that he gave his only

> begotten Son, that whosoever believeth in him
> should not perish, but have everlasting life.
>
> — JOHN 3:16

> The Lord is not slack concerning his promise, as
> some men count slackness; but is longsuffering
> to us-ward, not willing that any should perish,
> but that all should come to repentance.
>
> — 2 PETER 3:9

We see God's will is to save ALL. It's God's will that everyone is saved! Praise God he wants us all!

But not everyone is saved. Why is that?

Because God has done His part, but like it or not, we have a part to do. We have a responsibility in this too. We have to make a decision to choose Jesus.

MAKE THE WORD OF GOD YOUR LORD

> I am jealous for you with a godly jealousy. I
> promised you to one husband, to Christ, so that I
> might present you as a pure virgin to him.
>
> — 2 CORINTHIANS 11:2 (NIV)

> Let us rejoice and be glad and give him glory! For
> the wedding of the Lamb has come, and his bride
> has made herself ready.
>
> — REVELATION 19:7 (NIV)

We are the bride of Christ. We see this throughout scripture and also through the references above. This is our connection to the Father. We are adopted as His children because we are the bride of Christ.

> For you did not receive the spirit of slavery to fall back into fear, but you have received the Spirit of adoption as sons, by whom we cry, Abba! Father!
>
> — ROMANS 8:15 (ESV)

We are His children because we became one with Christ through marriage. We are adopted children. A marriage is made up of vows and commitments. They show forth our love towards our spouse.

> If ye love me, keep my commandments.
>
> — JOHN 14:15

You might ask…what does that have to do with your salvation?

When you confessed Jesus as Lord of your life, you made a promise to follow His word. He isn't just your Savior, He is LORD, and He is also the Word. That makes the Word of God your Lord.

> In the beginning was the Word, and the Word was with God, and the Word was God. He was in the beginning with God.
>
> — JOHN 1:1-2 (ESV)

> And the Word became flesh and dwelt among us, and we beheld His glory, the glory as of the only begotten of the Father, full of grace and truth.
>
> — JOHN 1:14

Do commandments matter? Let's ask the rich young ruler Jesus spoke with…

> And, behold, one came and said unto him, Good Master, what good thing shall I do, that I may have eternal life?
> And he said unto him, Why callest thou me good? there is none good but one, that is, God: but if thou wilt enter into life, keep the commandments.
> He saith unto him, Which? Jesus said, Thou shalt do no murder, Thou shalt not commit adultery, Thou shalt not steal, Thou shalt not bear false witness,
> Honour thy father and thy mother: and, Thou shalt love thy neighbour as thyself.
> The young man saith unto him, All these things have I kept from my youth up: what lack I yet?
> Jesus said unto him, If thou wilt be perfect, go and sell that thou hast, and give to the poor, and thou shalt have treasure in heaven: and come and follow me.
> But when the young man heard that saying, he went away sorrowful: for he had great possessions.
>
> — MATTHEW 19:16-22

We understand through this scripture that we must live according to Christ's word if we love Him and want to inherit eternal life.

Here is where the confusion comes in with many believers. We are not saved by works, however, choosing not to sin is a decision, not a work.

Let me say that again: choosing not to sin is a decision, NOT a work.

So we are right in saying we are not saved by our works, here is that scripture…

> For by grace are ye saved through faith; and that not of yourselves: it is the gift of God: Not of works, lest any man should boast
>
> — EPHESIANS 2:8-9

Remember, salvation is a decision. We are not talking about how to become saved when talking of sin. We are talking of the dreaded subject of walking away from salvation.

We are here to do the works of God and let Him work through us. Choosing not to sin is a decision, just like accepting Jesus. Sinning is a work. We can't hold sin in one hand and salvation in the other. We have to give that to God, so He can work through us. It's His works that save us; it's our works that condemn us. We can't live according to our works anymore; they lead to death. We live according to the Holy Spirit to be holy by allowing Him to work through us.

> For it is God which worketh in you both to will and to do of his good pleasure.
>
> — PHILIPPIANS 2:13

> For the wages of sin is death, but the gift of God is eternal life in Christ Jesus our Lord.
>
> — ROMANS 6:23

We work sin. God works salvation. To receive God's work for us, we have to decide to turn our backs on the works of sin and serve Him. For instance: when one commits adultery, they do not accidentally do it, they make a decision, and then they do the work of sin.

> Let no man say when he is tempted, I am tempted of God: for God cannot be tempted with evil, neither tempteth he any man: But every man is tempted, when he is drawn away of his own lust, and enticed.
> Then when lust hath conceived, it bringeth forth sin: and sin, when it is finished, bringeth forth death.
>
> — JAMES 1:13-15

There is no accidental sin. Every sin is a work based on a decision one has made to disobey God's word.

It is our decisions that will determine our destiny.

What if we sin? We can get it right, but only through repentance. We put this fresh sin we have committed under the blood of Jesus Christ. Only sin UNDER THE BLOOD, is forgiven sin.

> And almost all things are by the law purged with blood; and without shedding of blood is no remission.
>
> — HEBREW 9:22

Only sin under the blood can be put in remission. The only way to put sin under the blood is to repent of it and turn your back on it.

In summary:

- We are saved through our decision to pledge Jesus as Lord.
- Our works produce sin. God's works produce salvation.
- It is God's work that saves us. It is our work that leads to destruction.
- We cannot work in sin and be of God.

Here are some further scriptures showing that anyone living a lifestyle of sin will not go to heaven:

> Or do you not know that the unrighteous will not inherit the kingdom of God? Do not be deceived: neither the sexually immoral, nor idolaters, nor adulterers, nor men who practice homosexuality, nor thieves, nor the greedy, nor drunkards, nor revilers, nor swindlers will inherit the kingdom of God.
>
> — 1 CORINTHIANS 6:9-10

But the fearful, and unbelieving, and the abominable, and murderers, and whoremongers, and sorcerers, and idolaters, and all liars, shall have their part in the lake which burneth with fire and brimstone: which is the second death.

— REVELATION 21:8

Whoever commits sin also commits lawlessness, and sin is lawlessness. And you know that He was manifested to take away our sins, and in Him there is no sin. Whoever abides in Him does not sin. Whoever sins has neither seen Him nor known Him.

Little children, let no one deceive you. He who practices righteousness is righteous, just as He is righteous. He who sins is of the devil, for the devil has sinned from the beginning. For this purpose the Son of God was manifested, that He might destroy the works of the devil. Whoever has been born of God does not sin, for His seed remains in him; and he cannot sin, because he has been born of God.

In this the children of God and the children of the devil are manifest: Whoever does not practice righteousness is not of God, nor is he who does not love his brother.

— 1 JOHN 3:4-10 (NKJV)

> Work at living in peace with everyone, and work at living a holy life, for those who are not holy will not see the Lord.
>
> — HEBREWS 12:4 (NLT)

> I am the vine, ye are the branches: He that abideth in me, and I in him, the same bringeth forth much fruit: for without me ye can do nothing. If a man abide not in me, he is cast forth as a branch, and is withered; and men gather them, and cast them into the fire, and they are burned.
>
> — JOHN 15:5-6

These are just a few of many scriptures, but I stated these because they clearly show what will lead to hellfire. We see through these scriptures that we can't live in a sinful state and belong to God. Ultimately, we want to know how this affects the believer's walk with Christ? Can you look at any of these things as a believer and say that you haven't turned your back on them?

Have you turned your sin over to Jesus, and are you seeking Him? If not, then repentance needs to take place.

A person committed adultery for years and then repented to God and surrendered their life to Him. After 5 years, they were tempted, got away from God, and began to live in adultery again. This person is not seeking to make it right and isn't repenting of their sin. If they die in this state, will they go to heaven?

> Now the Spirit expressly says that in later times some will depart from the faith by devoting themselves to deceitful spirits and teachings of demons.
>
> — 1 TIMOTHY 4:1 (ESV)

Notice that some believers decide to depart from the faith. If there is one thing we can see through all of these scriptures it's this: Choosing sin, is rejecting Jesus.

We are the bride of Christ. Choosing to live in sin is equivalent to cheating on our vows. This results in a broken covenant. Jesus is willing to forgive us, but we must rededicate our lives to Him through repenting of our sin once again.

You mean to tell me that I need to ask God for forgiveness and turn away from my sin every time I do something wrong?" I don't mean to tell you anything BUT THAT.

> Then asked they him, What man is that which said unto thee, Take up thy bed, and walk?
> And he that was healed wist not who it was: for Jesus had conveyed himself away, a multitude being in that place.
> Afterward Jesus findeth him in the temple, and said unto him, Behold, thou art made whole: sin no more, lest a worse thing come unto thee.
>
> — JOHN 5:12-14

We ought to live our lives as if sin can send us to hell. The serpent (Satan) convinced Eve that she'd never die for eating a fruit, and so she ate it, not taking God's word seriously. In doing so, she brought a curse on all of mankind and caused us to naturally be predestined for a hell that wasn't made for us.

We don't want to make the same mistake again. We want to take sin seriously because it separates us from God. If we let it, it will do so eternally, should we have any sin we held on to when we enter eternity. So long as we are alive, we have grace and the ability to get it right. But when we leave this world, we will have judgement.

> He who overcomes shall be clothed in white garments, and I will not blot out his name from the Book of Life; but I will confess his name before My Father and before His angels.
>
> — REVELATIONS 3:5

Ask yourself, what happens if we don't overcome our sin and the Devil in life?

According to the scriptures, only the one who overcomes will not have their name blotted out of the Lamb's Book of Life.

What if we don't overcome?

We overcome through repentance and by God's work being shed abroad in our hearts.

11

CAN I LOSE MY SALVATION?

> Now the Spirit speaketh expressly, that in the latter times some shall depart from the faith, giving heed to seducing spirits, and doctrines of devils;
>
> — 1 TIMOTHY 4:1

No one can take salvation from you. However, you can walk away from your covenant with Christ.

Many walk away from Christ by choosing to continue to live in sin. We are the bride of Christ (Revelation 9). Understanding this gives us the knowledge and understanding that we are God's children because we are in covenant with Christ.

Jesus said those who love Him keep his commands (John 14:15). He further describes what happens to those who do not keep His commands in Matthew 7 and in Revelation 21 (among many other scriptures throughout the New Testament).

While many believe you can't lose salvation, as sure as you can choose to sin, you can choose to walk away from your covenant with Christ. If you are not His faithful bride, you will not know the Father.

> But he that shall endure unto the end, the same shall be saved.
>
> — MATTHEW 24:13

> He who overcomes shall be clothed in white garments, and I will not blot out his name from the Book of Life; but I will confess his name before My Father and before His angels.
>
> — REVELATION 3:5

Many will depart. Some will not endure, and some will not overcome. These are prerequisites of being with the Lord Jesus Christ. We can't do it alone, but through seeking the Holy Spirit, God empowers us to become His children.

> But as many as received him, to them gave he power to become the sons of God, even to them that believe on his name.
>
> — JOHN 1:12

12

WHAT IS HOLINESS?

> Follow peace with all men, and holiness, without which no man shall see the Lord.
>
> — HEBREWS 12:14

Holiness can only come as a gift from God Himself because we cannot attain it on our own in our fallen state. This is why Jesus had to come. He wants to restore us to holiness through the Holy Spirit.

Because of sin, we were unable to be the temples of the Holy Spirit as we were created. But when Jesus died, the physical temple (which housed the Holy Spirit) was torn at the veil, and the Holy Spirit came to us (Acts Chapter 2) and has never left us, just as Jesus promised in John 16.

Through Christ's blood, we are re-born (John 3:3-5), and we become holy because we are born again of the Spirit of God.

> And such were some of you. But you were washed, you were sanctified, you were justified in the name of the Lord Jesus Christ and by the Spirit of our God.
>
> — 1 CORINTHIANS 6:11 (NKJV)

Many love to quote scriptures like this, "As the scriptures say, There are none righteous—not even one."

This is true as originally quoted in Psalms, but when you become saved, you are born again. The old you is dead. Now Christ is the One living through you (Galatians 2:20). Is Christ righteous? We know without a doubt He is.

It is also our responsibility as believers to stay holy. We are no longer subject to the power of sin as believers, and if we do sin, we have an advocate we can take our sin to and release it.

As believers, we cannot live in a state of sin and belong to God. God's children have been cleansed from sin and don't live in it any longer. Our pursuit is no longer to please self; it is now to please our Heavenly Father because we love Him. His presence is better than the pleasure of sin, and it doesn't add sorrow to your life!

13

WHAT IS THE BAPTISM OF THE HOLY GHOST?

> Know ye not that ye are the temple of God, and that the Spirit of God dwelleth in you?
>
> — 1 CORINTHIANS 3:16-17

The baptism of the Holy Ghost began on the day of Pentecost in Acts Chapter 2 as prophesied by Jesus before He ascended and as He spoke in John Chapter 16.

This is described as an endowment of power in the Bible. The Holy Spirit came upon people in the Old and New Testament up until Jesus ascended. When He left, the Holy Spirit didn't come upon anyone anymore. He came to live within us. This is called the baptism of the Holy Spirit.

In John Chapter 3, you read of the born-again experience. Many will contend that this means you are baptized in the Spirit upon salvation. You are born of the Spirit when you get saved; being born of the Spirit is not the same as being baptized in the Spirit.

In John Chapter 4, Jesus met a woman at a well, and He told her that if she asked Him, He would give her a well within her springing up into everlasting life. This encounter is speaking of salvation. When Jesus saves you, you have a well of everlasting life within you. You are going to go to heaven. You belong to God.

However, Jesus didn't want you to stop at merely a well that springs up within you. Listen to this scripture...

> He that believeth on me, as the scripture hath said, out of his belly shall flow rivers of living water.
>
> — JOHN 7:38

Here we observe a difference between the initial spring within a believer and a river flowing out of a believer.

The baptism of the Holy Spirit will take what is in you (the Holy Spirit) and manifest God's power into the world. Like a river flowing from your inward well, this is an inward baptism that comes from the overflow of the Holy Spirit. You become bold, you become full of faith, you do whatever your heart leads you to do from listening to the Holy Spirit, so that you may be in His presence as often as possible.

Acts 19 describes that the baptism of the Holy Spirit and the act of salvation are two separate occurrences. While some do receive the baptism of the Holy Spirit upon salvation, it is a separate occurrence. It can happen much later in a walk with Christ than at the initial point of salvation. This shows that there are more sides to God and more to learn about Him than we will ever know at one time.

He may call us to be His child but later bring us to maturity as a powerful son or daughter by baptizing us in His Spirit. However, the Spirit baptism is for every believer and is to be sought. It will do what a phone booth did for Clark Kent for a man.

If you want to walk in the power that the apostles and the disciples of old walked in, and even some of our predecessors walked in, you must begin first through salvation and then immediately through the pursuit of the Holy Spirit baptism.

Although many do not teach how to receive the Holy Spirit, it is as easy as listening to what He is telling you and obeying him. All baptisms of the Holy Spirit happen with the signifying evidence of speaking in an unknown tongue. Even if it may sound foolish to you, if you hear a language within you, no matter how few in words it may be, yield to it. Open your mouth and speak what you feel to speak.

Healings happen, but not without laying on of hands and declaration of healing. There is an act of obedience to the Holy Spirit contingent upon all of the moves and workings of the Holy Spirit. Ask Him to speak to you so you can speak in tongues and know you are baptized in His Spirit.

I have had testimonies of church members who received the baptism in their bed at night, some in their vehicles during the daytime. It doesn't really matter where you are; it only matters that you yield to God.

God wants to teach us that the secret to walking in the power of His Spirit isn't a secret at all. There isn't any formula. There is only obeying what His Word says and what His Spirit says. When you do, signs and wonders always follow.

14

WHAT IS SPEAKING IN TONGUES?

There are three types of tongues.

PRAYING IN THE SPIRIT

> Likewise the Spirit also helpeth our infirmities: for we know not what we should pray for as we ought: but the Spirit itself maketh intercession for us with groanings which cannot be uttered.
>
> — ROMANS 8:26

The first one is praying in the Holy Ghost. This often happens when in prayer or in a state of worship. This is a prayer language. This does not need interpretation as it is not a message for the congregation; it is a prayer.

This builds your faith. It communicates to God things you need that you don't know you need. Ultimately, it is something that will happen when intensely seeking God or when pursuing God in a deepened state. The Spirit knows what we don't. We have to let Him speak.

> Praying always with all prayer and supplication in the Spirit, and watching thereunto with all perseverance and supplication for all saints;
>
> — EPHESIANS 6:18

> But ye, beloved, building up yourselves on your most holy faith, praying in the Holy Ghost,
>
> — JUDE 1:20

> For if I pray in an unknown tongue, my spirit prayeth, but my understanding is unfruitful. What is it then? I will pray with the spirit, and I will pray with the understanding also: I will sing with the spirit, and I will sing with the understanding also.
>
> — 1 CORINTHIANS 14:14 & 15

BAPTISM OF THE HOLY SPIRIT

> When the day of Pentecost arrived, they were all together in one place. And suddenly there came from heaven a sound like a mighty rushing wind, and it filled the entire house where they were sitting. And divided tongues as of fire appeared to them and rested on each one of them. And

> they were all filled with the Holy Spirit and began to speak in other tongues as the Spirit gave them utterance.
>
> — ACTS 2:1-4 (ESV)

This is the initial speaking in tongues that happens when every believer receives the immersive baptism of the Holy Spirit. This is the fulfillment of God's power in a believer. It turns the spring in you into a well flowing out of you.

In Acts Chapter 2, on the day of Pentecost, while many nationalities heard them speak in tongues, there was no interpreter. They just understood the message. That's the miracle of it. While this can come with interpretation, it does not have to. This is the baptism, not the gift.

> While Peter was still speaking these words, the Holy Spirit fell upon all those who heard the word.
> And those of the circumcision who believed were astonished, as many as came with Peter, because the gift of the Holy Spirit had been poured out on the Gentiles also. For they heard them speak with tongues and magnify God.
>
> — ACTS 10:44-46 (NKJV)

> When they heard this, they were baptized in the name of the Lord Jesus. And when Paul had laid hands on them, the Holy Spirit came upon them, and they spoke with tongues and prophesied. Now the men were about twelve in all.
>
> — ACTS 19:5-7 (NKJV)

THE GIFT OF TONGUES

> to another the working of miracles, to another prophecy, to another the ability to distinguish between spirits, to another various kinds of tongues, to another the interpretation of tongues.
>
> — 1 CORINTHIANS 12:10

This is concerning giving a message, not praying, in tongues. The gift of tongues is a sign for the unbeliever. While you can speak in tongues in church as a message, another may not give the interpretation they receive, and that is unfruitful. However, you shouldn't rely on someone else's obedience to determine your obedience.

This is why Paul is saying pray for the interpretation or pray for prophecy because prophecy edifies the body while the gift of tongues does not.

Ultimately, if God prompts you to do something, flow through the gift. God will provide interpretation.

> Pursue love, and earnestly desire the spiritual gifts,

especially that you may prophesy. For one who speaks in a tongue speaks not to men but to God; for no one understands him, but he utters mysteries in the Spirit. On the other hand, the one who prophesies speaks to people for their upbuilding and encouragement and consolation. The one who speaks in a tongue builds up himself, but the one who prophesies builds up the church. Now I want you all to speak in tongues, but even more to prophesy. The one who prophesies is greater than the one who speaks in tongues, unless someone interprets, so that the church may be built up. Now, brothers, if I come to you speaking in tongues, how will I benefit you unless I bring you some revelation or knowledge or prophecy or teaching?

— 1 CORINTHIANS 14:1-6 (ESV)

> Therefore, one who speaks in a tongue should pray that he may interpret. For if I pray in a tongue, my spirit prays but my mind is unfruitful. What am I to do? I will pray with my spirit, but I will pray with my mind also; I will sing praise with my spirit, but I will sing with my mind also. Otherwise, if you give thanks with your spirit, how can anyone in the position of an outsider say "Amen" to your thanksgiving when he does not know what you are saying? For you may be giving thanks well enough, but the other person is not being built up. I thank God that I speak in tongues more than all of you. Nevertheless, in church I would rather speak five words with my mind in order to instruct others, than ten thousand words in a tongue.
>
> — 1 CORINTHIANS 14:13-19 (ESV)

> Thus tongues are a sign not for believers but for unbelievers, while prophecy is a sign not for unbelievers but for believers. If, therefore, the whole church comes together and all speak in tongues, and outsiders or unbelievers enter, will they not say that you are out of your minds? But if all prophesy, and an unbeliever or outsider enters, he is convicted by all, he is called to account by all, the secrets of his heart are disclosed, and so, falling on his face, he will worship God and declare that God is really among you.
>
> — 1 CORINTHIANS 14: 22-25 (ESV)

15

WHAT ARE THE GIFTS OF THE SPIRIT?

But the manifestation of the Spirit is given to every man to profit withal.
For to one is given by the Spirit the word of wisdom; to another the word of knowledge by the same Spirit;
To another faith by the same Spirit; to another the gifts of healing by the same Spirit;
To another the working of miracles; to another prophecy; to another discerning of spirits; to another divers kinds of tongues; to another the interpretation of tongues:
But all these worketh that one and the selfsame Spirit, dividing to every man severally as he will.

— 1 CORINTHIANS 12:7-11

When you are baptized with the Holy Spirit, you receive access to the gifts of the Spirit. Each of these gifts are not grown or cultivated, they are given. God gives them at His will. However, the Bible describes seeking out the best gifts (1 Corinthians 12:31). The "best gift" as described, is the one that is needed at the time. For instance, a man who cannot walk doesn't need a gift of prophecy; he needs the gift of healing. Walking in the gifts of the Spirit and desiring the best gift would inspire a believer to command healing in the body of the lame man, and if unable to heal, to seek out the scriptures to obtain the gift or to grow in faith into a level that can conquer the enemy in that specific need.

God will not deny you a gift. He doesn't desire to give any child favoritism as the Bible describes. We just have to be mature enough in our faith to learn how to grow in faith.

While faith is a gift of the Spirit, it is also a fruit of the Spirit. Modern translations like to take faith and turn it into "faithfulness", but nonetheless, faith has to grow.

We are given a measure of faith, but it must be grown through obedience and boldness to receive the best gifts.

> I press toward the mark for the prize of the high calling of God in Christ Jesus.
>
> — PHILIPPIANS 3:14

There is a pressing and a pursuing that is involved with working in the gifts of the Spirit and the operation of the power of God.

16

WHAT IS THE FRUIT OF THE SPIRIT?

> But the fruit of the Spirit is love, joy, peace, longsuffering, gentleness, goodness, faith, meekness, temperance: against such there is no law.
>
> — GALATIANS 5:22-23

There is a vast difference between fruit and gifts; fruit is grown, gifts are simply given.

Many modern-day Christians tend to focus on what they can grow or cultivate. This pertains to and includes the fruit of the Spirit. All fruit must be cultivated. Fruit grows and is grown. It is God's will that we do everything in the fruit of the Spirit. You may not have much long-suffering and temperance when you first become saved, but through the Holy Spirit you grow. You may not have the ability to live constantly in a state of peace and joy, but through the Holy Spirit you learn how to grow. We are not meant to stay in a stagnate state, we are meant to grow in the Spirit into a place where the fruit of the Spirit not only sustains our spirit, but we can afford to bear fruit for others. We can be sowers of the fruit of the Spirit into other people's lives, but to do so, we have to address the state of our own spiritual fruit. We have to approach our life in the spirit intentionally and directly. There are no passive fruit bearers in the body of Christ! If we are going to bear fruit we have to start sowing into our daily lives with an approach, through faith, that intends to produce.

All fruit must be cultivated. You have to protect your fruit from ungodly consumers. Don't surround yourself with people doing things against the fruit of the Spirit. Get around others who take being a Christian in their lifestyle very seriously, so that you will also.

17

HOW DO I DEAL WITH DIFFICULT SITUATIONS IN LIFE?

…casting all your care upon Him, for He cares for you.

— 1 PETER 5:7 (NKJV)

Come unto me, all ye that labour and are heavy laden, and I will give you rest. Take my yoke upon you, and learn of me; for I am meek and lowly in heart: and ye shall find rest unto your souls. For my yoke is easy, and my burden is light.

— MATTHEW 11:28-30

God expresses in His Word that we should bring all of our cares to Him. We are not meant to deal with the difficulties of life alone. We are created to walk in authority and dominion in every situation we face. That's why the Bible expresses in John 16 that Jesus came to send us a helper, the Holy Spirit, to help us walk in the godly way that we are meant to.

We are the light of the world (John 1). This means we are not reactors - we are emitters. We don't follow the pace - we set the pace. It is God's will that we do not react to situations emotionally; we react to situations with faith and the Word of God.

Jesus expressed in the Bible that in this world we will have tribulation (John 16:33), but then it expresses for us to be of good cheer, for Christ has overcome the world. Galatians 2:2 says that Christ now lives within us.

Jesus, the overcomer, lives within us. We should take joy when we go through things. Rough times are opportunities for miracles. It is only through trials that we see the power of God made manifest in our lives. This is how we become who God has called us to be and do what God has called us to do. We don't run from trouble; we face trouble. We overcome trouble.

Always remember this…what is in you is greater than what is in front of you. You may have tribulation, but tribulation will never have you.

If you face a mountain, speak to your mountain and tell it to move!

Bring your burdens to the Lord and speak His Word. Do what His Word says in spite of how you feel. God's way always brings victory.

18

HOW DO I OVERCOME AN ADDICTION?

> I can do all things through Christ who strengthens me.
>
> — PHILIPPIANS 4:13

The most important advice I can give anyone is to never give up when dealing with addictions.

The key to deliverance is complete surrender. It is impossible to give God your everything and stay the same. Addictions are often manifestations tied to things in our life that we refuse to let go of.

Addiction is not a root; it's a fruit.

Getting down deep into the personal areas of your life and giving them to God will cause more freedom in your life than you thought you could have ever experienced. Ask God to remove anything from your life that would cause you to stay addicted, and He will. Pray earnestly.

Stay committed to laying it down, and you will. God promises those who seek Him will find Him. He can set you free in an instant! We just have to open our heart and allow Him to take out the root.

19

HOW DO I DEAL WITH TEMPTATION?

Now when the tempter came to Him, he said, If You are the Son of God, command that these stones become bread. But He answered and said, It is written, Man shall not live by bread alone, but by every word that proceeds from the mouth of God.
Then the devil took Him up into the holy city, set Him on the pinnacle of the temple, and said to Him, "If You are the Son of God, throw Yourself down. For it is written: He shall give His angels charge over you,' and, 'In their hands they shall bear you up, Lest you dash your foot against a stone.'" Jesus said to him, "It is written again, 'You shall not tempt the Lord your God.'"
Again, the devil took Him up on an exceedingly high mountain, and showed Him all the kingdoms of the world and their glory. And he said to Him, "All these things I will give You if You will fall down and worship me." Then Jesus said to him,

> "Away with you, Satan! For it is written, 'You shall worship the Lord your God, and Him only you shall serve.'"
>
> Then the devil left Him, and behold, angels came and ministered to Him.
>
> — MATTHEW 4:3-11 (NKJV)

Everyone faces temptation—even Jesus was tempted.

Never allow yourself to feel guilty for being tempted. There is a difference between having a thought and dwelling on a thought.

Satan will always try to tempt you with things that he believes will be appealing to you. Remember that Satan can't read your thoughts. He doesn't know what's in your mind. He can only judge how you will act based on what comes out of your mouth.

Let your speech be filled with authority. Speak scriptures. Refuse the enemy and rebuke him whenever a thought comes your way that doesn't line up with God's will. Whenever you recognize a thought that is from the enemy, begin to physically do things that are in the opposite direction of the temptation.

Take it to God! Rebuke the enemy immediately and pray, and the Bible says that Satan will have to flee from you.

20

WHAT ARE THE BENEFITS OF LIVING FOR CHRIST?

The blessing of the Lord, it maketh rich, and he addeth no sorrow with it.

— PROVERBS 10:22

There are so many benefits to being a believer. You will experience the favor and blessing of God without sorrow. Because Jesus fulfilled the law as He said He would (Matt. 5:17), you receive the blessing of the fulfilled law described in Deuteronomy 28…

> Now it shall come to pass, if you diligently obey the voice of the Lord your God, to observe carefully all His commandments which I command you today, that the Lord your God will set you high above all nations of the earth.
> And all these blessings shall come upon you and

overtake you, because you obey the voice of the
   Lord your God:
"Blessed shall you be in the city, and blessed shall
   you be in the country.
"Blessed shall be the fruit of your body, the produce
   of your ground and the increase of your herds,
   the increase of your cattle and the offspring of
   your flocks.
"Blessed shall be your basket and your kneading
   bowl.
"Blessed shall you be when you come in, and blessed
   shall you be when you go out.
"The Lord will cause your enemies who rise against
   you to be defeated before your face; they shall
   come out against you one way and flee before
   you seven way:
"The Lord will command the blessing on you in your
   storehouses and in all to which you set your
   hand, and He will bless you in the land which the
   Lord your God is giving you.
"The Lord will establish you as a holy people to
   Himself, just as He has sworn to you, if you keep
   the commandments of the Lord your God and
   walk in His ways.
Then all peoples of the earth shall see that you are
   called by the name of the Lord, and they shall be
   afraid of you.
And the Lord will grant you plenty of goods, in the
   fruit of your body, in the increase of your
   livestock, and in the produce of your ground, in
   the land of which the Lord swore to your fathers
   to give you.

> The Lord will open to you His good treasure, the
> heavens, to give the rain to your land in its
> season, and to bless all the work of your hand.
> You shall lend to many nations, but you shall not
> borrow.
> And the Lord will make you the head and not the
> tail; you shall be above only, and not be beneath,
> if you heed the commandments of the Lord your
> God, which I command you today, and are
> careful to observe them.
> So you shall not turn aside from any of the words
> which I command you this day, to the right or the
> left, to go after other gods to serve them.
>
> — DEUTERONOMY 28:1-14

God gives you all authority over Satan's devices in your life such as sin, sickness, and every spirit that causes those types of things.

> Behold, I give you the authority to trample on
> serpents and scorpions, and over all the power of
> the enemy, and nothing shall by any means
> hurt you.
>
> — LUKE 10:19 (NKJV)

> And I will give you the keys of the kingdom of
> heaven, and whatever you bind on earth will be
> bound in heaven, and whatever you loose on
> earth will be loosed in heaven.
>
> — MATTHEW 16:19 (NKJV)

These are just the beginning of his promises. The Bible is a written will for the believer, filled with God's promises for us. The more you read the Word, the more you understand that it is and always will be God's intention to bless those who walk according to His purpose.

The best benefit, however, is to know God personally as your Father. You become His child and you will spend eternity with Him, in this life and in the life to come!

21

WHAT IS MY PURPOSE?

Before I formed you in the womb I knew you;
>   Before you were born I sanctified you; I ordained
>   you a prophet to the nations.

>   — JEREMIAH 1:5 (NKJV)

For God does not show favoritism.

>   — ROMANS 2:11 (NLT)

"For I know the plans I have for you," declares the
>   LORD, "plans to prosper you and not to harm
>   you, plans to give you hope and a future."

>   — JEREMIAH 29:11 (NKJV)

Understanding God's will for your life comes with also understanding that His purpose for you didn't start after birth. As He told Jeremiah, He also has known you and foreordained you for your purpose specifically in the time that you live in. You are not accidentally here or living in the wrong place or time. God ordained your life for a purpose from heaven and He knew who He wanted you to be before you were born. He designed you with the gifts, talents and desires for His purpose in you to be completed on the earth.

> Neither shall they say, Lo here! or, lo there! for, behold, the kingdom of God is within you.
>
> — LUKE 17:21 KJV

Understand that God's will is to establish His kingdom on the earth. He uses men and women to do that by creating us with a portion of His kingdom within us. Without the pursuit of God's Spirit, His kingdom can't be poured out and won't be established. This is why it is important to not only become saved but to begin to pursue God's plan for your life and sell out to it.

> And he gave some, apostles; and some, prophets; and some, evangelists; and some, pastors and teachers; For the perfecting of the saints, for the work of the ministry, for the edifying of the body of Christ: Till we all come in the unity of the faith, and of the knowledge of the Son of God, unto a perfect man, unto the measure of the stature of the fullness of Christ:
>
> — EPHESIANS 4:11-13

Every single person on the earth has a calling that falls into one of these five categories. Many folks feel that their calling is their job or raising their children. This is not true at all. You can rule out anything as your call that doesn't have eternal significance; if it mattered before you were here, it will matter after you leave. It is like grabbing the baton in a race and taking it to the next runner. You have a part to play in this, but it is bigger than any one person.

Walking in your purpose is also not the same thing as pursing a gift. The Bible says that your gift will make room for you (Proverbs 18:16). This means that you may be the best singer or performer in the world, but that is merely a gift. The gift builds the platform that purpose will walk out on. If you are a singer, sing to the best of your ability. Give it your all. It will be a platform for the Gospel message in you, but it is the message that is the purpose - not the gift. In some way, we will all walk in the capacity of the 5-fold ministry, if we are truly seeking to do God's will for our lives.

JACOB ENGLISH

THE GREAT COMMISSION

> And Jesus came and spake unto them, saying, All power is given unto me in heaven and in earth. Go ye therefore, and teach all nations, baptizing them in the name of the Father, and of the Son, and of the Holy Ghost: Teaching them to observe all things whatsoever I have commanded you: and, lo, I am with you always, even unto the end of the world. Amen.
>
> — MATTHEW 28:18-20

The Great Commission is the epitome of the purpose that lies within every believer. It is meant to spread the Gospel news to every person we can and not only bring them into salvation, but also into a purpose of their own ordained by the Father.

22

HOW DO I IMPLEMENT GOD'S WILL INTO MY LIFE DAILY?

> We can make our plans, but the LORD determines our steps.
>
> — PROVERBS 16:9 (NLT)

Let me answer this question with another question. If you were judged on your commitment to Christ by your daily walk, did you live today in a way that would be pleasing to God?

As a rule of thumb, I have always read a chapter of the Bible three times a day, once more than I feed my body daily. I want my spirit to be stronger than my flesh. I often start the day with one chapter of Proverbs (there are thirty-one, one for each day) and one chapter of Psalms. I will then read a New Testament chapter and an Old Testament chapter throughout the day, unless I feel impressed by the Holy Spirit to read something specific. It may seem repetitive, it may seem redundant, but reading and re-reading God's Word instills the knowledge of His will in you, which will empower you to face your adversary on a daily basis. If you don't know where to start, start at the beginning of the New Testament at lunch and the beginning of the Old Testament after dinner.

The first thing I do every morning is pray. I consider this my "first fruits" of the day. If I ever forget or don't have time set aside, maybe I'm running late to an appointment, then I excuse myself to the restroom and I pray there or I pray at lunch, but I never miss my prayer time. I pray for my family. I pray for my church and my church members. I pray for those whom the Lord leads across my path that I have not been connected to yet. I pray for ministry. I pray for all who the Lord lays on my heart. However, the most important thing I pray is that I am covered by the blood of Jesus Christ. I surrender my life to Christ every morning to accomplish His will for that day. I ask him to remove anything that could hinder me from His will and to lead me into His perfect will for this day. I also ask Him to fill me to overflowing with His presence every day. I don't know of a single day that I have spent seeking Him, that His presence didn't touch me within that day. You can feel God's presence every day!

Your Christian walk is made up of your daily and weekly routine. If you are going to get close to God, start with setting a plan that you meet every single day.

I suggest fasting at least one meal (not breakfast) a week. Replace it with prayer and reading God's Word.

Keep a godly daily routine, and you will never backslide! God wants to bless you every day, so make yourself available to Him every day.

23

IS IT ALWAYS GOD'S WILL TO DELIVER AND HEAL?

Beloved, I wish above all things that thou mayest prosper and be in health, even as thy soul prospereth.

— 1 JOHN 1:12

When talking about salvation, deliverance or healing, many people don't understand that the word "salvation" in the Bible references all three things.

This is why there are instances in the Bible where Jesus asked if it would be better for Him to tell a crippled man that his sins were forgiven or to rise and take up his bed and walk? They are the same miracle. The one who is saved is also meant to be healed and delivered.

I know this because the word "salvation" in the Bible comes from the Greek "sozo". "Sozo" is the trifecta of total salvation, meaning to be saved, delivered, and healed all at one time. This word addresses the healing of one's soul from sin (salvation), the healing of one's iniquities or addictions (delivered) and the healing of one's body (healing) all at once.

Just as sure as it is God's will that all would be saved, it is equally His will that all would be healed and delivered.

This scripture gives clear definition to the separation of prosperity and health in body and soul, and how it is God's will for all of the "beloved" (believers) to not only be healthy, but to prosper.

There are so many scriptures concerning God's will that lead to a greater understanding of authority for the believer over sin, addiction, sickness, and disease. So many that I can't quote them all.

Here's a safe way to identify God's will: If it wasn't around before sin happened and it's not going to be in heaven, it's safe to say that it isn't God's will and it came from sin.

Jesus defeated sin, and now He lives in you! All of the effects of sin have been overcome. You are healed, you are delivered, and you are SAVED in Jesus' name!

24

IS IT GOD'S WILL FOR ME TO PROSPER?

"For I know the plans I have for you," declares the LORD, "plans to prosper you and not to harm you, plans to give you hope and a future."

— JEREMIAH 29:11 (NKJV)

Beloved, I wish above all things that thou mayest prosper and be in health, even as thy soul prospereth.

— 3 JOHN 2:2

We can see throughout the scriptures that it is God's will to bless us. The scripture shown in 3 John 2 reveals that it is God's will for us to prosper specifically in health, in soul, and in our present state. God has John separate these three things because it is often said by many Christians that when God says it's His will to prosper you, He is speaking of inward prosperity. This scripture descriptively separates health, inward prosperity, and financial prosperity. God expresses His will that we not only prosper in one area of life, but in every area of life. Prosperity furthers the Gospel.

We never look at healing and say that it is God's will to heal us inwardly but not outwardly. In the same case, we often, as full gospel believers, say the opposite thing about finances. We have to hold the same standard for prosperity as for healing. It's either all metaphoric or it's all literal. We know through the life of Christ that while He taught in parables, He healed in a very literal manner. So also, He prospers us both inwardly in faith and outwardly in the finances of one who yields their finances to Him and pursues financial growth to grow the kingdom through faith.

As we see in the scriptures, prosperity is without a doubt God's will for the believer.

25

WHAT IS A TITHE AND WHY DOES IT MATTER?

> Will a man rob God? Yet ye have robbed me. But ye say, Wherein have we robbed thee? In tithes and offerings. Ye are cursed with a curse: for ye have robbed me, even this whole nation. Bring ye all the tithes into the storehouse, that there may be meat in mine house, and prove me now herewith, saith the Lord of hosts, if I will not open you the windows of heaven, and pour you out a blessing, that there shall not be room enough to receive it. And I will rebuke the devourer for your sakes, and he shall not destroy the fruits of your ground; neither shall your vine cast her fruit before the time in the field, saith the Lord of hosts. And all nations shall call you blessed: for ye shall be a delightsome land, saith the Lord of hosts.
>
> — MALACHI 3:8-12

Tithe is translated as a tenth. It was instituted by the first fruits offering given by Abel and Cain and then again well defined by Abraham with Melchizedek.

All blessings of God require that you give yourself completely for God to bless you. Tithe, although only a tenth represents the giving of your entire finances to God through faith. If you don't give tithe, God can't bless your finances. In refusing your tithe, you allow the enemy to doubly curse your finances and steal from you. Have you ever wondered why you seem to constantly run out of money in your life? Savings and budgets have nothing to do with it. Tithing is the key to protecting your finances.

If you ever want to be blessed or increased or prosperous in your financial life, you must pay tithe. Without tithe, your finances will be cursed. It doesn't matter how good of a preacher or a Christian you may be; without giving your tithe you don't fully belong to God.

The act of an offering outside of tithe is giving in faith and belief for increase. I hate when preachers or ushers say things like, "We aren't giving to receive anything, we are just giving because we love You." That's not scriptural at all.

> Give, and it shall be given unto you; good measure, pressed down, and shaken together, and running over, shall men give into your bosom. For with the same measure that ye mete withal it shall be measured to you again.
>
> — LUKE 6:38

When you give, as soon as you pay your tithe and release your offering in the offering plate you should begin to thank God and declare increase over your finances in expectation. That's what the scriptures declare over you. Give expecting to receive, and you will. Don't let go of a blessing just because modern-day churches frown on it. Let them keep frowning. You should be determined to be blessed.

26

HOW DO I PRAY?

So He said to them, "When you pray, say:
Our Father in heaven,
Hallowed be Your name.
Your kingdom come.
Your will be done
On earth as it is in heaven.
Give us day by day our daily bread.
And forgive us our sins,
For we also forgive everyone who is indebted to us.
And do not lead us into temptation,
But deliver us from the evil one.

— LUKE 11:2-4 (ESV)

Prayer is not made up of trying to be heard or to sound like a good orator in church. It's also not about repetition. Prayer is about reverently speaking to your Father in faith and truth. That's who He is, your Heavenly Father. Reverence Him in prayer and give glory to His name first and foremost, but it is His will that you bring every care to Him.

Prayer should always be done in faith. This means if you are feeling sad, don't say "God I'm sad." Instead say, "Father, I thank You that Your Word says that in Your presence is fullness of joy. I thank You for Your presence right now. I thank You that my joy is full."

Never let sadness or depressive thoughts come out of your mouth. Satan doesn't know your thoughts. He may try to inject a thought or a temptation but he has no way of knowing if it's having an effect on you unless you speak it. It's very important not to speak outside of faith, especially in prayer.

Prayer should be an act of praise, thanks, and yielding. Don't cry and beg God. God responds to faith. Speak in faith; he's a God of faith and not a God of emotionalism.

Pray that God's will is done in you and in those around you. Pray that God establishes His kingdom through you on the earth. Tell Him that you belong to Him and that you yield to His will in your life. Thank Him for protection and that He has given you power over sin, temptation, and evil.

Beyond that, listen to the Holy Spirit. He may prompt you to pray for a person or against the enemy in an area of someone's life.

The lines of communication should always be open to God. Say what you need to say to Him and reverence Him, but spend the rest of the day listening to His Word through preaching, singing and studying so that He can speak to you and answer your prayers by bringing His presence into your life. He wants to be with you every day. Make room for Him!

27

WHAT IS FAITH?

> Now faith is the substance of things hoped for, the evidence of things not seen.
>
> — HEBREWS 11:1

Faith is substance. There is nothing in the realm of the spirit that will be done without faith. Whether someone recognizes it or not, we all have faith. Both believers in Christ and those who don't believe in Him have made a decision to either put their faith in Jesus or to put it in themselves.

As a substance, faith becomes what a believer sees in the scripture and hopes for. Faith takes shape through declaration and action. When we speak a thing in faith and pursue it through our actions, this substance called faith begins to take shape until the manifestation of our hope comes to fruition. Faith literally becomes what we believe for. It is important not to stop speaking and taking action when what you are believing for doesn't happen initially.

Faith doesn't fail. We just have to remember not to be weary in well-doing. Keep doing things in faith until they happen. By faith you can move mountains!

We can see this by reading Hebrews 11. It declares that God framed the world through faith. He took faith, declared things into existence, and faith became what He declared. We cannot do the works of God without faith. Faith is the key to all things spiritual. The Bible declares that it is impossible to please God without faith.

Faith has another side, also referred to as evidence. The Bible declares that Satan is our accuser. With this knowledge, we can see that Satan is like an evil lawyer accusing us of all things anti-faith. But when you begin to speak in faith through belief in the scriptures, you present evidence to him and to God that he is a liar and that you are what the Bible declares. Without declaration and representation of the scriptures through faith, there is nothing to present contrary to the Devil's accusations as evidence. That is why many "believe" for healing but never get healed or delivered. There must be a declaration and an action of evidence that is displayed in faith. Without the evidence, you don't win the case. With the evidence, you always win the case. Show your evidence today! Declare your faith, and don't stop declaring it and taking action towards it until faith takes shape in your situation.

28

CALL TO REPENTANCE: BENEDICTION

> The LORD has appeared of old to me, saying: "Yes,
> I have loved you with an everlasting love;
> Therefore with lovingkindness I have drawn you.
>
> — JEREMIAH 31:3

I pray that this book gives direct insight into the foundational questions of our faith. God wants us all to be equipped and able to spread the Gospel of Jesus Christ with unwavering faith. If you've read this book and you wonder if the Gospel of Jesus Christ is for you, I want to tell you that without a doubt, it's for you.

Jesus loves you, and He wants to accomplish great things with you. He is merely waiting on you to fully give your life to Him.

If you've read this book and you feel as though you are lacking in some areas and you'd like for God to make you whole today, I'd like for you to speak this prayer over yourself with heartfelt intent:

Jesus, I love you.
I don't want to live the way I've been living anymore. I'm sorry that I've sinned against you.
I ask you to forgive me and take away all of my sins right now.
I ask that you change my desires from what I have wanted into what You want for me.
I want to accomplish Your plan for my life.
I don't want to feel empty anymore. I want to be made whole.
I confess You as my Lord.
Fill me up. Make me new.
I ask that You break every connection, addiction and sickness that would hinder my faith in You or try to lead me astray.
I ask that You'd put angels around me to protect me from Satan's plan against me.
I ask that You would send Your Holy Spirit to baptize me and fill me with Your power.
I thank You, Lord Jesus, that every old part of me has passed away and I am brand new.
From this day forward I'll do as You show me to do.
I'm Yours fully and completely.
In Jesus' name, Amen!

If you prayed that prayer with me, I want to tell you that your name was just written down in a book in heaven called the Lamb's Book of Life. You are now on your way to heaven!

I implore you to get into a Spirit-filled church and get connected with like-minded believers. It's God's will for you to do incredible things! And you will, in Jesus' name.

ABOUT THE AUTHOR

Jacob English was trained in the spirit in an independent Pentecostal ministry and is a fifth generation preacher. Raised in the quaint southern town of Barnesville Georgia, he has traveled and ministered since being a teenager and has been in ministry in some form his whole life. Jacob began doing tent revivals during the lockdowns for Covid19 in 2020. As most churches were closing, he didn't want to stop assembling with believers. Through the leading of the spirit, He felt to start pastoring a church. He currently pastors a church in Reynolds Georgia with his wife and son, called Living Faith Church which he started in July 2021. When not writing, he is tending to daily ministry duties, doing ministry podcasts, recording gospel music or spending quality time with his family. His pastimes still involve gaming and going to the gym.

Keep in touch with Jacob via the web:

www.thelivingfaithchurch.com

Email: livingfaithreynolds@gmail.com

facebook.com/jacob.m.english

www.ingramcontent.com/pod-product-compliance
Lightning Source LLC
Chambersburg PA
CBHW051348040426
42453CB00007B/472